Love Letters from Goa

To God's Mighty Warriors

Transcribed by Theresa Heflin

~Book Two~

Llumina
Christian
Books

ISBN: 1-59526-469-8 HC
      1-59526-468-X PB
      1-59526-470-1 E-book

Printed in the United States of America by Llumina Christian Books

Library of Congress Control Number: 2006907191

Contents

Note: All scriptures are copied from QuickVerse 2006

Dedication

I dedicate this book to

The Hope Center in Waverly, Tennessee

Acknowledgments

I want to start with thanking God our Father, Jesus, His Son, and the Holy Spirit. It is my belief that these letters are from God, inspired by the Holy Spirit, and our redemption is through Jesus. Thank you, my Lord, my Savior, my Friend.

Secondly, I want to thank Craig Stevens, Michael Moore, and Dave Ott. The wonderful website
http://www.westbrookstevens.com/theresa_heflin.htm
is designed by them. I also appreciate your encouragement. I am looking forward to your second book in your Geronimo Stone series!

I thank each one who has contributed to this book with your comments – whether on the back of this book or in the sections at the on-line book stores.

I want to thank all of my family and friends. I am who I am because of you. Whether I fail or succeed, you have always been in my life cheering me on, laughing with me, crying with me, and loving me with all your heart. I love you my sisters, Sharon, Brenda, and Nichole! I love you mom and pops! I love you Allison & Stephen and Missy and Gene! I thank you for my wonderful grandchildren…Parker, John and Stephen, Jr.

I love you Andy, Michelle, T.J., Kaci, and Andrew. I love you Matt, Shanna, Faith, Drew, Colton, Gracie, and Hope. I love you, Jaybird, Cori, Jamie, Brittany, Elizabeth, and Emily Rose. I love you Casey, Christy, Devyn and Avery. You will always have a big chunk of my heart. God has truly blessed you, Ralph.

Pastor Josh Hannah, I love you and Jessica and your entire congregation at Friendship World Outreach! Our Lord has blessed me greatly by sending me to your church to work with all of you for His Kingdom. To all my other friends and family, please know that you are just as loved and important to me! I wish I could name you all! I thank you Father God for all my blessings of love from your precious people, in Jesus Name, Amen.

Foreword

The opportunity arose for me to step out in faith on a greater level when my husband died on February 10, 2002. Although it was an opportunity that I would not have chosen, God has been faithful to me. He has filled me with a deep peace during the loneliest times of my life.

To fill the lonely minutes, hours, and days, I began to search the Bible through various Bible studies. After completing all of the Beth Moore studies, and reading Rick Warren's books, I became acquainted with Henry Blackaby's *Experiencing God.* Through *Experiencing God,* I learned of Avery Willis' *MasterLife,* a study on discipleship. It seemed that the more I learned, the more I wanted. The *MasterLife* workbooks offer a section at the end of each daily study to write down what you sense God is saying to you. This was so new to me that as I began writing what I sensed God was saying, the sentences came out short and choppy. I was like a child learning how to do something new. But, as I began to settle into the comfort of writing what I sensed God was saying, my walk with Christ grew into a deeper level of knowing the oneness of a relationship with our Creator.

As I am reading and editing this book two, I am in the middle of writing book seven. I am amazed at how God has blessed me with His loving words. I believe God's words are for all of us to help us during times of sorrow and healing, tests and trials. The words are an encouragement to me and I believe they will encourage you too throughout our daily walk on this earth until He calls us home.

I would like to invite you to come with me into a deeper place of love and peace as we begin to realize that we have just begun to know the true love of God for his priceless, precious treasure…us.

Fifty-One

PSALM 119 NKJV

[17] Deal bountifully with Your servant,
That I may live and keep Your word.
[18] Open my eyes, that I may see
Wondrous things from Your law.
[19] I *am* a stranger in the earth;
Do not hide Your commandments from me.
[20] My soul breaks with longing
For Your judgments at all times.
[21] You rebuke the proud—the cursed,
Who stray from Your commandments.
[22] Remove from me reproach and contempt,
For I have kept Your testimonies.
[23] Princes also sit *and* speak against me,
But Your servant meditates on Your statutes.
[24] Your testimonies also *are* my delight
And my counselors.

Theresa Heflin

Letter Fifty-One

Oh mighty warrior, My mighty warrior, My treasure, My priceless treasure — now is the time for greater things! Oh — watch what I can do! Oh — see Me working among you! My Glory has come to rest on you, precious one who represents Me. I give you all My love — I give you My power! I give you blessings beyond what you can imagine! Oh how I have waited for this day! I am here among you. Rest in Me — sing to Me, My love! Rejoice! For the Victory is won! Oh, mighty warrior, the one whom I have chosen — shine for Me! Keep your eyes on Me. I will reveal myself to you. I hear you, precious one — I hear your cries, I count each tear. I cry with you, mighty warrior. I am here — I am with you. Never doubt My love for you. Never doubt — obey My every command — only then can you rest. I give you blessings filled with love, laughter, joy and great peace. Oh mighty warrior — I am smiling on you. I am pleased with you — My creation — My beautiful one — you serve Me well.

Fifty-Two

PSALM 119 NKJV

[25] My soul clings to the dust;
Revive me according to Your word.
[26] I have declared my ways, and You answered me;
Teach me Your statutes.
[27] Make me understand the way of Your precepts;
So shall I meditate on Your wonderful works.
[28] My soul melts from heaviness;
Strengthen me according to Your word.
[29] Remove from me the way of lying,
And grant me Your law graciously.
[30] I have chosen the way of truth;
Your judgments I have laid *before me.*
[31] I cling to Your testimonies;
O LORD, do not put me to shame!
[32] I will run the course of Your commandments,
For You shall enlarge my heart.

Theresa Heflin

Letter Fifty-Two

Your heart was breaking that day. You did not know the plans I had for you. I sent you My chosen one to bring you relief. Your spirit was full of anguish, full of despair, full of sorrow. I came to you, oh precious one, and gave you a refreshing drink from My waters. Oh one that I love, it was not time. But I was with you. I was watching over you closely. I never took My eyes off of you. I have always protected you from the evil one. I have great plans in store for you. For you love Me completely and trust Me solely and depend on Me for your every breath. Oh how I have longed for this day with you. Oh how I have waited and watched over you. I created you for this time. My great peace rests on you – for you know My voice. You recognize Me – oh – you recognize Me! I sing to you My love – I rejoice over you, mighty warrior! I Am Your God who sings to you! Oh hear Me sing My love songs to you! I Am Your God who loves you so.

𝔉𝔦𝔣𝔱𝔶-𝔗𝔥𝔯𝔢𝔢

PSALM 119 NKJV

33 Teach me, O LORD, the way of Your statutes,
And I shall keep it *to* the end.
34 Give me understanding, and I shall keep Your law;
Indeed, I shall observe it with *my* whole heart.
35 Make me walk in the path of Your commandments,
For I delight in it.
36 Incline my heart to Your testimonies,
And not to covetousness.
37 Turn away my eyes from looking at worthless things,
And revive me in Your way.
38 Establish Your word to Your servant,
Who *is devoted* to fearing You.
39 Turn away my reproach which I dread,
For Your judgments *are* good.
40 Behold, I long for Your precepts;
Revive me in Your righteousness.

Theresa Heflin

Letter Fifty-Three

Oh precious one, I commune with you all the time. I talk to you all the time. I drink in every time you whisper I love you. Oh how I love to hear your whispers to Me. I drink from your words of love to Me with great pleasure, for I am in love with you. Oh worship Me – adore Me – beloved love of Mine. Oh how I love to hear you praise Me. Oh how I love to hear you love Me. Oh, mighty warrior of Mine – you love Me with such beauty! You are My beautiful one. You are the one I have chosen. You are the one that I love, you are My prized possession. Oh let your roots go deep in Me – for I am filling you with all of Me. I am completely saturating you in My powerful love. My love – the power of My love – the love that will sustain you – the love that gives you strength – the love that brings great peace – the love that overcomes all the evil. Oh let Me love you more! Cry out for more! Oh how I love to answer you! Come with Me – I will take you there.

Fifty-Four

PSALM 119 NKJV

41 Let Your mercies come also to me, O LORD—
Your salvation according to Your word.
42 So shall I have an answer for him who reproaches me,
For I trust in Your word.
43 And take not the word of truth utterly out of my mouth,
For I have hoped in Your ordinances.
44 So shall I keep Your law continually,
Forever and ever.
45 And I will walk at liberty,
For I seek Your precepts.
46 I will speak of Your testimonies also before kings,
And will not be ashamed.
47 And I will delight myself in Your commandments,
Which I love.
48 My hands also I will lift up to Your commandments,
Which I love,
And I will meditate on Your statutes.

Theresa Heflin

Letter Fifty-Four

I watch you through the night. Oh I watch you closely in the night. Oh how My heart rejoices when you wake every morning with your sweet whispers of love to Me. Oh, mighty warrior, never doubt My love for you - I long to hear you. I love listening to you tell Me you love Me. I love your adoration and sweet words of love to Me. Oh how I love to hear you praise Me! Oh worship Me, My love – praise My Holy Name – for I am smiling on you. You refresh Me with your worship, My creation, My mighty warrior. Oh I am so pleased with you. Oh how I love you so. You are a fountain springing forth! Oh refresh My world, precious one. Let them drink from My fountains in you. They are thirsty, mighty warrior – they are hungry, precious one. Oh let them drink deeply of My love! Oh feed them My Word – My Everlasting Word! My Word will release them from the darkness, My love. Remain in Me, precious one. Drink deeply from My love so that you may give My love to My people. Oh My precious people – they need Me so. You serve Me well, mighty warrior – I am pleased with you.

𝔉ifty-𝔉ive

PSALM 119 NKJV

[49] Remember the word to Your servant,
Upon which You have caused me to hope.
[50] This *is* my comfort in my affliction,
For Your word has given me life.
[51] The proud have me in great derision,
Yet I do not turn aside from Your law.
[52] I remembered Your judgments of old, O LORD,
And have comforted myself.
[53] Indignation has taken hold of me
Because of the wicked, who forsake Your law.
[54] Your statutes have been my songs
In the house of my pilgrimage.
[55] I remember Your name in the night, O LORD,
And I keep Your law.
[56] This has become mine,
Because I kept Your precepts.

Theresa Heflin

Letter Fifty-Five

You lay open your heart before Me. You come to Me with your requests. I answer each one. I do not turn away from any request. I am always at work answering you. My ways are different from your ways. My timing is perfect, precious one. I answer you with much love and caring. Do not be frustrated in serving Me. For I see you loving Me. I see you obeying My every command. My Word is true — do not doubt, mighty warrior! I am blessing you and I am at work among you. Keep your eyes on only Me, My love, My treasure — for you cannot do this without Me. You cannot survive without Me. You cannot live in peace and joy apart from Me. Do not be discouraged, one that I love. I am leading you. I am guiding you. I am in control of your every thought. Listen to My words of love to you. I sing My blessings over you — for I rejoice in you with much joy! Oh how I rejoice over you. You please Me, mighty warrior. Never doubt — never forget — I am here — I am with you — I am at work among you. Bare open your heart before Me and watch what I can do! See Me work in the hearts of those who adore Me! Trust only Me, precious one. I Am The Truth. I Am Your Only Way. Remain in Me — for I long to give you more!

Fifty-Six

PSALM 119 NKJV

[57] *You are* my portion, O LORD;
I have said that I would keep Your words.
[58] I entreated Your favor with *my* whole heart;
Be merciful to me according to Your word.
[59] I thought about my ways,
And turned my feet to Your testimonies.
[60] I made haste, and did not delay
To keep Your commandments.
[61] The cords of the wicked have bound me,
But I have not forgotten Your law.
[62] At midnight I will rise to give thanks to You,
Because of Your righteous judgments.
[63] I *am* a companion of all who fear You,
And of those who keep Your precepts.
[64] The earth, O LORD, is full of Your mercy;
Teach me Your statutes.

Theresa Heflin

Letter Fifty-Six

Oh mighty warrior, I am with you. I am here walking among you, precious one. I am opening doors. You are entering with great peace and joy. Oh praise Me, precious one! Oh how I love to hear you praise Me. You are My love – My creation – in whom I am well pleased. Oh tender heart, I love you so. Remain open to Me, My love. I pour My love into your heart that is open before Me. There is power in My love. There is strength in My love. There is encouragement in My love. There is much joy in My love. Your heart is filled with My peace. Oh mighty warrior, do not be afraid – for I am with you. I go before you – I prepare the hearts for you. I Am Your God who blesses you for you obey Me and you serve Me well. Oh precious one, the power of My love is in you. Go forth in Victory! Go forth in songs of praise to Me. Oh how I drink from your praises. Your praises are refreshment to Me. I am in love with you, mighty warrior – never forget – I love you so…and I Am God Almighty, Creator of heaven and earth!

𝔉ifty-𝔖even

PSALM 119 NKJV

[65] You have dealt well with Your servant,
O Lord, according to Your word.
[66] Teach me good judgment and knowledge,
For I believe Your commandments.
[67] Before I was afflicted I went astray,
But now I keep Your word.
[68] You *are* good, and do good;
Teach me Your statutes.
[69] The proud have forged a lie against me,
But I will keep Your precepts with *my* whole heart.
[70] Their heart is as fat as grease,
But I delight in Your law.
[71] *It is* good for me that I have been afflicted,
That I may learn Your statutes.
[72] The law of Your mouth *is* better to me
Than thousands of *coins of* gold and silver.

Theresa Heflin

Letter Fifty-Seven

I am filling you with wisdom and insight, mighty warrior. I am preparing you and equipping you for greater things. I am tending to you with much love and care. Oh how precious you are to Me. Oh how I love to watch you obey Me! Oh how I love your open heart laid bare before Me. I have planned these things before you and watch your delight with much pleasure. Oh how I delight in you, My love! Oh how you smile for Me! Oh how you sing to Me! I am all you need, precious one that I love. Remain completely in Me for I love you so. I am all around you watching you closely – sending you out – loving you deeply – blessing you richly – in all of My goodness. I Am Good, mighty warrior! Never fear or worry over anything. I am at work all around you. Keep your trust in only Me for I will take you down the right paths. The paths I take you on are filled with much joy and delight! Oh mighty warrior, I am so pleased with you. I rejoice over you, My love. I love you so.

Fifty-Eight

PSALM 119 NKJV

⁷³ Your hands have made me and fashioned me;
Give me understanding, that I may learn Your commandments.
⁷⁴ Those who fear You will be glad when they see me,
Because I have hoped in Your word.
⁷⁵ I know, O LORD, that Your judgments *are* right,
And *that* in faithfulness You have afflicted me.
⁷⁶ Let, I pray, Your merciful kindness be for my comfort,
According to Your word to Your servant.
⁷⁷ Let Your tender mercies come to me, that I may live;
For Your law *is* my delight.
⁷⁸ Let the proud be ashamed,
For they treated me wrongfully with falsehood;
But I will meditate on Your precepts.
⁷⁹ Let those who fear You turn to me,
Those who know Your testimonies.
⁸⁰ Let my heart be blameless regarding Your statutes,
That I may not be ashamed.

Theresa Heflin

Letter Fifty-Eight

I will surround you with My chosen ones, righteous one. I protect you, I guard you, no evil can harm you – no evil can touch you – for I Am God – and you are Mine! The decree has been spoken! The Creator of all heaven and earth loves you, protects you, and delights in you! The price is paid! The Victory is won! Oh mighty warrior, I am so pleased and filled with delight as I rejoice over you – for you love Me so! Oh how I love to see you love Me so! Never doubt – never fear – for I Am Your God who watches you closely. I am in control, mighty warrior! I am doing all things, precious one. Worship Me, praise Me, adore Me – oh how I love to hear you praise Me! Keep your eyes heavenward. Do not look on the circumstances of this earth – look to Me! I am sending you, precious one. Some will reject you – oh, but some will come. Oh, bring them to Me – for I love them so. Do not be discouraged, mighty warrior – for many will come! Keep looking to Me for your help – your strength – your joy, and your great peace. For I give them to you with much joy and pleasure. Never forget, precious one – you are special and I love you so!

Fifty-Nine

PSALM 119 NKJV

⁸¹ My soul faints for Your salvation,
But I hope in Your word.
⁸² My eyes fail *from searching* Your word,
Saying, "When will You comfort me?"
⁸³ For I have become like a wineskin in smoke,
Yet I do not forget Your statutes.
⁸⁴ How many *are* the days of Your servant?
When will You execute judgment on those who persecute me?
⁸⁵ The proud have dug pits for me,
Which *is* not according to Your law.
⁸⁶ All Your commandments *are* faithful;
They persecute me wrongfully;
Help me!
⁸⁷ They almost made an end of me on earth,
But I did not forsake Your precepts.
⁸⁸ Revive me according to Your loving kindness,
So that I may keep the testimony of Your mouth.

Theresa Heflin

Letter Fifty-Nine

Yes – I say yes to you! You are My mighty warrior in whom I am well pleased. I am blessing everything you do. You will prosper in everything you touch. I am with you. I am leading you – for you trust only Me. Oh mighty warrior – you will see Me do things that will thrill your soul! You will watch Me with utter amazement. I enjoy delighting you! Oh how delightful you are, My child, My love, My obedient one. It is My pleasure to bless you – for you love Me so – and you thank Me from your heart. I love you, mighty warrior! Oh how I love you so. I enjoy watching you. I see you – I smile on you. I rejoice over you, precious one that I have chosen. Always keep your eyes on only Me. You will go in great peace. You will know My voice. Do not worry, My love – do not fret – you will know. I will not leave you to wonder. I will tell you – I will show you. I will take you – I take you personally. I am with you. You are in My presence at all times. My presence goes with you. You will always be able to feel My presence – for I will never leave you – never. Rest in Me – remain in Me – I Am Your God who loves you.

Sixty

PSALM 119 NKJV

[89] Forever, O Lord,
Your word is settled in heaven.
[90] Your faithfulness *endures* to all generations;
You established the earth, and it abides.
[91] They continue this day according to Your ordinances,
For all *are* Your servants.
[92] Unless Your law *had been* my delight,
I would then have perished in my affliction.
[93] I will never forget Your precepts,
For by them You have given me life.
[94] I *am* Yours, save me;
For I have sought Your precepts.
[95] The wicked wait for me to destroy me,
But I will consider Your testimonies.
[96] I have seen the consummation of all perfection,
But Your commandment *is* exceedingly broad.

Theresa Heflin

Letter Sixty

My commandments are true. From the beginning of time until the end – My commandments are true – never doubt – never waiver – obey each one – for it is good for you! Follow My instructions carefully and you will have great peace and joy. Oh mighty warrior – do not dread the morrow. I am with you, precious one. I am in control. You will see My wonders this week. You will dance in joy – for the Victory is won! I bring great peace and joy from My vast storehouse in heaven. You will radiate My peace, My great peace. It will spill out and rest on them – they will delight in My presence. Always remember – never forget – I Am God Almighty, Creator of all of heaven and earth! All things submit to Me. Oh precious one – this is but a small thing for Me. I Am Your King who loves you. I protect you from the evil one. Sing to Me – praise My Name – for My Victorious Mighty Right Hand rests on you. Go in peace. I give you My great peace. Go in love – love My people – My precious people.

Sixty-One

PSALM 119 NKJV

[97] Oh, how I love Your law!
It *is* my meditation all the day.
[98] You, through Your commandments, make me wiser than my enemies;
For they *are* ever with me.
[99] I have more understanding than all my teachers,
For Your testimonies *are* my meditation.
[100] I understand more than the ancients,
Because I keep Your precepts.
[101] I have restrained my feet from every evil way,
That I may keep Your word.
[102] I have not departed from Your judgments,
For You Yourself have taught me.
[103] How sweet are Your words to my taste,
Sweeter than honey to my mouth!
[104] Through Your precepts I get understanding;
Therefore I hate every false way.

Theresa Heflin

Letter Sixty-One

I fill you with wisdom and insight – I fill you with understanding, mighty warrior. I answer your cries for more – for you walk in Me – you obey Me – you hunger for more of Me. I do not turn away from your requests. I answer you with much love and delight. I will reveal Myself to you. Oh how you will see Me! You will delight in the fullness of My joy! Oh precious one that I love – I see you searching My Holy Word. I watch you study to know more of Me. Oh how I love to watch you! I know your tender heart. You lay it open for Me to search you. I search you – I take out what will harm you – I fill it with My pure, holy, deep peace. You are so full of My peace – you do not miss what I have taken out that would hurt you. Oh how I love your trust in Me. Oh how it thrills Me to hear you whisper – "I trust you Lord – I trust you Lord!" Oh precious one – never tire of telling Me – for I love to hear you tell Me – oh how I enjoy your praises to Me. Worship Me – adore Me – oh how I smile upon you – oh how I bless you – I am so pleased with your tender heart – My creation – My beautiful creation. I give you all of My love – love My people – oh love My precious people! They are so dear to Me! Bring them into My Kingdom – love them – I give you your love for them.

Sixty-Two

PSALM 119 NKJV

[105] Your word *is* a lamp to my feet
And a light to my path.
[106] I have sworn and confirmed
That I will keep Your righteous judgments.
[107] I am afflicted very much;
Revive me, O LORD, according to Your word.
[108] Accept, I pray, the freewill offerings of my mouth, O LORD,
And teach me Your judgments.
[109] My life *is* continually in my hand,
Yet I do not forget Your law.
[110] The wicked have laid a snare for me,
Yet I have not strayed from Your precepts.
[111] Your testimonies I have taken as a heritage forever,
For they *are* the rejoicing of my heart.
[112] I have inclined my heart to perform Your statutes
Forever, to the very end.

Theresa Heflin

Letter Sixty-Two

Oh precious one, you have just begun to see what I can do. Oh how I love to delight you! God Almighty – Creator of all of heaven and earth is at work among you. I bless you! I come with great peace and joy. Let all of heaven rejoice and sing for the ones, the precious ones that are entering into My Kingdom! I love you, mighty warrior! I rejoice with you. I sing with you. Oh praise Me, My love – for I Am All Things Wonderful and Good. I Am Your God who loves you so. Continue in your love – never tire of loving My precious people. I will give you strength for each new day. I give you great peace and joy for each new day. Oh sing to Me – one that I love. I am with you, mighty warrior. I am watching you closely. You are safe. I keep you safe in the shelter of My wings. I cover you with My feathers. Rest in Me – rest, precious one – I am tending to all your needs.

Sixty-Three

PSALM 119 NKJV

[113] I hate the double-minded,
But I love Your law.
[114] You *are* my hiding place and my shield;
I hope in Your word.
[115] Depart from me, you evildoers,
For I will keep the commandments of my God!
[116] Uphold me according to Your word, that I may live;
And do not let me be ashamed of my hope.
[117] Hold me up, and I shall be safe,
And I shall observe Your statutes continually.
[118] You reject all those who stray from Your statutes,
For their deceit *is* falsehood.
[119] You put away all the wicked of the earth *like* dross;
Therefore I love Your testimonies.
[120] My flesh trembles for fear of You,
And I am afraid of Your judgments.

Theresa Heflin

Letter Sixty-Three

You will not lose hope. You know My voice. Do not worry, precious one — you have been faithful before when opposition struck you. You will stand firm — for you know Me intimately. I Am Your King who watches over you with tender mercy and care. Never forget — I am with you. My Victorious Mighty Right Hand rests on you, precious one that I love. Go in peace — go — for I have given you great peace. I am the one you turn to for your strength. I am the one you turn to for your joy. I am the one you turn to for your great peace. Oh how I fill you full to overflowing. You have all My blessings resting on you. The Holy Spirit of Almighty God hovers over you. My angels surround you — I am with you. Never forget — it is I and I have overcome, My love! I Am Your God who loves you. The Creator of heaven and earth goes before you.

Sixty-Four

1 JOHN 5 NKJV

[3]For this is the love of God, that we keep His commandments. And His commandments are not burdensome. [4]For whatever is born of God overcomes the world. And this is the victory that has overcome the world—our faith. [5]Who is he who overcomes the world, but he who believes that Jesus is the Son of God?

[14]Now this is the confidence that we have in Him, that if we ask anything according to His will, He hears us. [15]And if we know that He hears us, whatever we ask, we know that we have the petitions that we have asked of Him.

Theresa Heflin

Letter Sixty-Four

I bless you with great faith, mighty warrior. This faith that I give you will sustain you. You will be strengthened by My Word which will bring forth great peace and joy. Do not doubt, precious one that I watch closely, I am with you. The Holy Spirit of the Living God hovers over you! Oh great man of God – you will come to know Me more! I choose to give you more – I choose to deliver you – you are My faithful one. Keep your eyes on only Me! Look only to Me! Go in faith – go in great faith – for I have come to deliver you. I Am Your Mighty King who loves you so. I protect you from the evil one. Never doubt – never doubt – I say to you, never doubt! Trust Me – trust Me completely – and see what I can do! Let Me take you deeper into Me! Obey Me – obey My every command – do not disobey Me.

Sixty-Five

PROVERBS 1 NKJV

⁷ The fear of the LORD *is* the beginning of knowledge,
But fools despise wisdom and instruction.

³³ But whoever listens to me will dwell safely,
And will be secure, without fear of evil."

PROVERBS 2 NKJV

⁶ For the LORD gives wisdom;
From His mouth *come* knowledge and understanding;
⁷ He stores up sound wisdom for the upright;
He is a shield to those who walk uprightly;
⁸ He guards the paths of justice,
And preserves the way of His saints.

Letter Sixty-Five

You refresh Me with your praises! I bless you in your praises to Me – then your refreshment comes. I want to bless you – I want to pour down My joy and laughter from heaven on you! I bring with Me My deep peace – peace that only I can give! Remain in Me. Let My Word enter you with the drink from My deep well of knowledge and wisdom. Oh cry out for wisdom and knowledge! Cry out for more! Let Me take you deeper – let Me bless you with the fullness of My love! Let Me bless you with great peace and the delightfulness of My joy and laughter. Oh let My light shine in My world! Stand out in love! Love My people – My precious people! Love them into My Kingdom! Let My Glory shine in you for the entire world to see! Sing to Me in the midst of your storm and watch Me roll the clouds away! Oh watch Me – My beautiful one that loves Me so. Praise My Name – worship Me – rest your cares on Me – I take good care of you – one that I love. You are the one who guides them into Me through My guiding light. Sing to Me – honor Me – let Me bless you – I love your praises – I drink from them and smile on you.

Sixty-Six

ISAIAH 65 NKJV

For as the days of a tree, *so shall be* the days of My people,
And My elect shall long enjoy the work of their hands.
²³ They shall not labor in vain,
Nor bring forth children for trouble;
For they *shall be* the descendants of the blessed of the LORD,
And their offspring with them.
²⁴ "It shall come to pass
That before they call, I will answer;
And while they are still speaking, I will hear.

Theresa Heflin

Letter Sixty-Six

Mighty warrior, oh My precious mighty warrior, I have been drinking in your praises and loving requests for My people – My precious people. I am saying yes to you! Every soul – I say yes to you – for you love Me so. Oh precious one who trusts Me – I am with you. I pour My great love into you – oh how I love to watch you serve Me. Oh how I give you your love more and more – you will know the fullness of Me. You will know the richness of Me. You will experience things you cannot begin to imagine – for I Am Your God who loves you so. I Am The Creator of All That Is – I can do whatever I choose! I choose to say yes to everything you ask of Me – for you seek My pleasure and My will – I bless you – I am with you – I will bring those that you love into My Kingdom! Oh how heaven rejoices for the souls entering into My Kingdom! Sing for Me – praise Me – oh how I love your praises – oh how I treasure your prayers and requests. They are very precious to Me. Ask Me always – I love to hear you ask Me. I do not weary of listening to you. I smile on you and I bless you with much joy and delight! Go in My Name – I will bless everything you say and do!

Sixty-Seven

ECCLESIASTES 3 NKJV

[1] To everything *there is* a season,
A time for every purpose under heaven:
[2] A time to be born,
And a time to die;
A time to plant,
And a time to pluck *what is* planted;
[3] A time to kill,
And a time to heal;
A time to break down,
And a time to build up;
[4] A time to weep,
And a time to laugh;
A time to mourn,
And a time to dance;
[5] A time to cast away stones,
And a time to gather stones;
A time to embrace,
And a time to refrain from embracing;
[6] A time to gain,
And a time to lose;
A time to keep,
And a time to throw away;
[7] A time to tear,
And a time to sew;
A time to keep silence,
And a time to speak;
[8] A time to love,
And a time to hate;
A time of war,
And a time of peace.

Theresa Heflin

Letter Sixty-Seven

Oh precious one that I love, it is well with your soul. I am pleased with you, My love. Your heart is tender before Me and you love My people – My precious people. I am with you, mighty warrior. My Spirit grieves with you. It is a time for weeping, My love. Oh one that I love – it is a refreshing drink to Me to watch you love My people. So many do not love and My heart aches for My lost people. I weep with you when My people do not love one another. These are the times when we weep, My love. Oh how I love you so. Remain in Me. Never tire of being My faithful servant. Never tire of loving My people! Oh how My people need My love! I pour My love into you – oh pour My love into them! Oh how precious you are to Me – you are My prized possession. I treasure you – I tenderly care for you – I bless you from My vast storehouses in heaven! Open your heart – lay it open before Me – I fill you completely. I cleanse you in My blood – you are Mine and I Am Yours – My precious garden – My radiant one. You glow in My love – oh one that I love – you are entering a deeper place in Me – we are one.

Sixty-Eight

2 CHRONICLES 20 NKJV

"Hear me, O Judah and you inhabitants of Jerusalem: Believe in the LORD your God, and you shall be established; believe His prophets, and you shall prosper." [21]And when he had consulted with the people, he appointed those who should sing to the LORD, and who should praise the beauty of holiness, as they went out before the army and were saying:

"Praise the LORD,
For His mercy *endures* forever."

[22]Now when they began to sing and to praise, the LORD set ambushes against the people of Ammon, Moab, and Mount Seir, who had come against Judah; and they were defeated.

Theresa Heflin

Letter Sixty-Eight

I have given you traveling mercy. I am with you — nothing will harm you — for My Mighty Right Hand covers you. I am giving you a time of refreshing. The workers are few, mighty warrior — and the time is short — remain in Me and do not look around you. Keep your eyes on only Me. Do not get discouraged for I am at work among you. It is harvest time, mighty warrior. Do not forget — the price is paid — the Victory is won! Look to Me for your every need and sing My praises. Let Me hear you trust Me. Let Me hear your faith with your songs of thankfulness to Me.

Sixty-Nine

PSALM 119 NKJV

¹²¹ I have done justice and righteousness;
Do not leave me to my oppressors.
¹²² Be surety for Your servant for good;
Do not let the proud oppress me.
¹²³ My eyes fail *from seeking* Your salvation
And Your righteous word.
¹²⁴ Deal with Your servant according to Your mercy,
And teach me Your statutes.
¹²⁵ I *am* Your servant;
Give me understanding,
That I may know Your testimonies.
¹²⁶ *It is* time for *You* to act, O LORD,
For they have regarded Your law as void.
¹²⁷ Therefore I love Your commandments
More than gold, yes, than fine gold!
¹²⁸ Therefore all *Your* precepts *concerning* all *things*
I consider *to be* right;

Letter Sixty-Nine

Rest in Me today — meditate on My commands — meditate on My blessings. Let Me fill you anew with My refreshing. I love you, mighty warrior — I am pleased with you. I smile upon you today and take you into Me — in a deeper place within Me. I want all of you today. I want all of your attention. I will not share you with the world today. Today is our time of loving — refreshing and blessings. I am strengthening you. I am not a hard taskmaster. My yoke is easy and My burden is light when you rest in Me, precious one. Pay close attention to Me today. I am giving you your thoughts. I am showing you My ways. I am teaching you something new today. Listen to My still small voice — for I am walking with you. I am talking with you. Oh how I love our alone times. I love to drink in your words of love to Me. I love to hear you love Me. I enjoy you — I delight in you — I bless you — oh how I bless you! You are My chosen one in whom I am well pleased. Today is our day — come.

Seventy

PSALM 119 NKJV

[129] Your testimonies are wonderful;
Therefore my soul keeps them.
[130] The entrance of Your words gives light;
It gives understanding to the simple.
[131] I opened my mouth and panted,
For I longed for Your commandments.
[132] Look upon me and be merciful to me,
As Your custom *is* toward those who love Your name.
[133] Direct my steps by Your word,
And let no iniquity have dominion over me.
[134] Redeem me from the oppression of man,
That I may keep Your precepts.
[135] Make Your face shine upon Your servant,
And teach me Your statutes.
[136] Rivers of water run down from my eyes,
Because *men* do not keep Your law.

Theresa Heflin

Letter Seventy

I love this time with you, precious one. Oh how I love our alone time to refresh you. I love when you turn to Me for your every need — for only I can fill your needs. I give you everything you need — I give you everything you want — for your desires are to please Me! I will give you all you want to please Me — I smile upon you, My love. I keep you close to My heart. I hold you close — you are under My watchful eye — no harm will come to you. You are Mine and oh I take care — good care — of My own! Never should you fear — never should you doubt My love for you. Never doubt My power — never — I say never doubt — for I Am God — Almighty God — Creator of all that is — I gave you My Son — He paid the price for you! Go forth rejoicing — for the Victory is won, mighty warrior! The Victory is won! I want to hear you worship Me. I want to hear you sing love songs to Me. Worship Me with all of your heart, mind, soul, body, and strength — for I Am Your God who loves you.

Seventy-One

PSALM 119 NKJV

[137] Righteous *are* You, O LORD,
And upright *are* Your judgments.
[138] Your testimonies, *which* You have commanded,
Are righteous and very faithful.
[139] My zeal has consumed me,
Because my enemies have forgotten Your words.
[140] Your word *is* very pure;
Therefore Your servant loves it.
[141] I *am* small and despised,
Yet I do not forget Your precepts.
[142] Your righteousness *is* an everlasting righteousness,
And Your law *is* truth.
[143] Trouble and anguish have overtaken me,
Yet Your commandments *are* my delights.
[144] The righteousness of Your testimonies *is* everlasting;
Give me understanding, and I shall live.

Theresa Heflin

Letter Seventy-One

Oh mighty warrior, I Am Faithful and True. You can depend on Me, precious one. I will never let you down. I am with you. I never leave you alone – ever! I hear you when you call on Me. I answer every request – for I Am Your God who loves you so. Lean on Me – I Am Your Strength – I Am Your Joy – I Am Your Peace – I Am Your Rest. I give you My blessings – trust Me for all your needs and see what I can do! I know your heart has questions – I know, My treasure – I know. I will bring to you understanding, wisdom, and insight. Remain in Me – continue seeking more – for I love to give you more. I will reveal Myself to you. I am in control, one that loves Me so – I am in control of all things. Trust Me completely – for I Am All You Need. I created the earth for you, My love. I walk among you on My earth – I enjoy you – I love you – I talk with you – you are My friend. Oh mighty warrior, I am so pleased with you.

Seventy-Two

PSALM 119 NKJV

[145] I cry out with *my* whole heart;
Hear me, O LORD!
I will keep Your statutes.
[146] I cry out to You;
Save me, and I will keep Your testimonies.
[147] I rise before the dawning of the morning,
And cry for help;
I hope in Your word.
[148] My eyes are awake through the *night* watches,
That I may meditate on Your word.
[149] Hear my voice according to Your loving kindness;
O LORD, revive me according to Your justice.
[150] They draw near who follow after wickedness;
They are far from Your law.
[151] You *are* near, O LORD,
And all Your commandments *are* truth.
[152] Concerning Your testimonies,
I have known of old that You have founded them forever.

Theresa Heflin

Letter Seventy-Two

I hear you, mighty warrior. I listen to your words — I open your heart — it lays open and bare before Me. I take all of your needs — all of your longings — all of your requests — I let them enter into Me — and I answer each one with all of the love of the One who is love — the Creator of all — I fill your heart with peace. I replace your worries with love — oh the love I give you — the love this world cannot give you. Only I can satisfy the longings — for I created you to yearn for Me — to long for Me — and I give you more and more. Oh come, enter into Me deeper. Let Me fill you with all of Me. Seek Me — cry out for wisdom and insight — I will not turn you away! As you seek Me, I run to you! I long for your complete love. I am here — come to Me — let Me fill you with the strength of My love. Let Me fill you with the joy of My love. Let Me fill you with the peace in My love. Oh come — I fill you to overflowing! I give you all of Me! Give My love to My people — oh My precious people — I love them so.

Seventy-Three

PSALM 119 NKJV

153   Consider my affliction and deliver me,
For I do not forget Your law.
154   Plead my cause and redeem me;
Revive me according to Your word.
155   Salvation *is* far from the wicked,
For they do not seek Your statutes.
156   Great *are* Your tender mercies, O LORD;
Revive me according to Your judgments.
157   Many *are* my persecutors and my enemies,
Yet I do not turn from Your testimonies.
158   I see the treacherous, and am disgusted,
Because they do not keep Your word.
159   Consider how I love Your precepts;
Revive me, O LORD, according to Your loving kindness.
160   The entirety of Your word *is* truth,
And every one of Your righteous judgments *endures* forever.

Letter Seventy-Three

Oh mighty warrior, My precious mighty warrior who loves Me so – oh how I love to speak to you – oh how I love to walk with you – oh how I love to listen to you – I answer you – oh I answer you – I love you so. You join Me, My love – we are one. You will weep with Me – you will feel My sorrow. You will laugh with Me and feel My joy. Oh sing to Me – praise Me – worship Me – adore Me – I long to hear you sing to Me. Your spirit will be revived in your praises to Me. Oh how I love the way you trust Me. Oh precious, priceless treasure of Mine – never doubt – never question My deep love for you. My love will never fail you. My love sustains you in the opposition. My full love is in you. Draw from My well, love of Mine. Draw deeply from My waters. Oh let them fill you with all of Me. Drink deeply, My love – drink deeply – for I am here. I have given you all of Me – take Me fully – I want all of you – I have given you all of Me. I bless you, mighty warrior – oh how you please Me. I am smiling on you – go in My love – go in My peace – go in My joy – for I am with you!

Seventy-Four

PSALM 119 NKJV

[161] Princes persecute me without a cause,
But my heart stands in awe of Your word.
[162] I rejoice at Your word
As one who finds great treasure.
[163] I hate and abhor lying,
But I love Your law.
[164] Seven times a day I praise You,
Because of Your righteous judgments.
[165] Great peace have those who love Your law,
And nothing causes them to stumble.
[166] LORD, I hope for Your salvation,
And I do Your commandments.
[167] My soul keeps Your testimonies,
And I love them exceedingly.
[168] I keep Your precepts and Your testimonies,
For all my ways *are* before You.

Theresa Heflin

Letter Seventy-Four

I purify you; I sanctify you in My blood. You are pure before Me. I welcome you into My holy place of worship – for you are My beloved. I listen to you there – I talk with you there – in My holy place of perfect love. Oh precious one in whom I am well pleased – I am with you. I am guiding you. I am leading you – I am preparing the way for you. I delight in you – I enjoy blessing you – I give you more and more – for I am strengthening you. Oh mighty warrior – I go before you – I surround you – I am at work among you. I never leave you. I protect you from the evil one – for you love My instructions – you love to obey Me – I love to bless the heart that obeys Me. Oh how I rejoice over your love for Me – I give you your love – I Am Your King who loves you so. I am pleased with your worship – I am pleased with your love. I am pleased with you, mighty warrior – oh how I am pleased with you. You are My chosen one – never fear – never doubt – I Am God – Almighty God – who gave My Son – My beloved Son to you. You are surrounded by all of Me! Go in peace – go in joy – give My precious people My love.

Seventy-Five

PSALM 119 NKJV

¹⁶⁹ Let my cry come before You, O LORD;
Give me understanding according to Your word.
¹⁷⁰ Let my supplication come before You;
Deliver me according to Your word.
¹⁷¹ My lips shall utter praise,
For You teach me Your statutes.
¹⁷² My tongue shall speak of Your word,
For all Your commandments *are* righteousness.
¹⁷³ Let Your hand become my help,
For I have chosen Your precepts.
¹⁷⁴ I long for Your salvation, O LORD,
And Your law *is* my delight.
¹⁷⁵ Let my soul live, and it shall praise You;
And let Your judgments help me.
¹⁷⁶ I have gone astray like a lost sheep;
Seek Your servant,
For I do not forget Your commandments.

Theresa Heflin

Letter Seventy-Five

You are close to My heart, mighty warrior. I am wrapped around you protecting you. I surround you with My magnificent love and power. No harm will touch you in My perfect love. Remain in Me for I Am Your God who loves you so. Obey My every command for you have been set free. I have set you free from all bondage. I have filled you to overflowing with My perfect peace. I send you out with the fullness of Me. I am guiding you in every step that you take. Pay close attention to Me, My love. I will not lead you down a wrong path. I am in control of all things. Keep your eyes on only Me. Trust only Me. My ways are not your ways. My ways are good for you. My ways bring health to you. My ways bring joy in your soul. My ways give you great peace. My ways are loving. I give you My love — My complete love. Give My love to My people — oh My precious people — I love them so. Help them, precious one that I love — love them into My Kingdom. I give you everything you need. Never doubt — never fear — I am with you always.

Seventy-Six

2 CHRONICLES 20

"Listen, all you of Judah and you inhabitants of Jerusalem, and you, King Jehoshaphat! Thus says the LORD to you: 'Do not be afraid nor dismayed because of this great multitude, for the battle *is* not yours, but God's. ¹⁷You will not *need* to fight in this *battle.* Position yourselves, stand still and see the salvation of the LORD, who is with you, O Judah and Jerusalem!' Do not fear or be dismayed; tomorrow go out against them, for the LORD *is* with you."

¹⁸And Jehoshaphat bowed his head with *his* face to the ground, and all Judah and the inhabitants of Jerusalem bowed before the LORD, worshiping the LORD. ¹⁹Then the Levites of the children of the Kohathites and of the children of the Korahites stood up to praise the LORD God of Israel with voices loud and high.

Theresa Heflin

Letter Seventy-Six

Remember the things I have done, mighty warrior. Remember the singers that went before Jehoshaphat's army. They sang to Me – oh they sang praises to Me and My Holy Splendor! They trusted Me – they believed Me – for I Am God! I let them live in peace when they put their trust in Me. I Am Your God who takes good care of you. Go forth singing praises to Me – oh how I love to hear you worship Me. The battle is Mine, mighty warrior – remember – the battle is Mine. I go before you – I Am Your Victorious King in your times of battle! I hear your cries – I see your trust – I delight in your praises – and I protect you, precious one that I love. Never take your eyes off of Me. Remain on the path that I take you – stand firm and praise My Name in the midst of all opposition, My armies go before you – My armies surround you! I Am Your Rear Guard – never forget My Mighty Power – My Victorious Mighty Right Hand rests on you. Oh how I love to fight for you while you sing to Me! I Am Your Covering – I love you so, mighty warrior – My mighty warrior – in whom I am well pleased.

Seventy-Seven

ACTS 8

[26]Now an angel of the Lord spoke to Philip, saying, "Arise and go toward the south along the road which goes down from Jerusalem to Gaza." This is desert. [27]So he arose and went. And behold, a man of Ethiopia, a eunuch of great authority under Candace the queen of the Ethiopians, who had charge of all her treasury, and had come to Jerusalem to worship, [28]was returning. And sitting in his chariot, he was reading Isaiah the prophet. [29]Then the Spirit said to Philip, "Go near and overtake this chariot."

[30]So Philip ran to him, and heard him reading the prophet Isaiah, and said, "Do you understand what you are reading?"

[31]And he said, "How can I, unless someone guides me?" And he asked Philip to come up and sit with him.

[39]Now when they came up out of the water, the Spirit of the Lord caught Philip away, so that the eunuch saw him no more; and he went on his way rejoicing. [40]But Philip was found at Azotus. And passing through, he preached in all the cities till he came to Caesarea.

Letter Seventy-Seven

Oh precious one who seeks to know Me more. I am here. I will show you. I will tell you. I have special plans for you. I have given you a special purpose. I am in control of you, My love. Do not worry – My timing is perfect and you will know. My love, I will not leave you to wonder – you will know. I want you to love Me – I want you to worship Me – I want you to adore Me – that is what pleases Me, My love. I will take care of all your needs. I send you – I go with you – I want all of your attention centered on only Me. I am guiding you. I bring people to you – I send you to people. I am in total control of you with great joy. I cherish our time. I am in love with you, mighty warrior. You know My voice. You know when I send you – you know the people I send to you – for we are one. We are in harmony – we are in tune – we are in perfect love and you know My great peace. You are very precious to Me and I tenderly care for you with all My love. I trust you with My people – My precious people that I love. Serve Me, My love – completely. I want all of you – at all times – I give you My love – give My love to My people – for that is My Perfect Will.

Seventy-Eight

1 SAMUEL 15 NKJV

[22]So Samuel said:
"Has the LORD *as great* delight in burnt offerings and sacrifices,
As in obeying the voice of the LORD?
Behold, to obey is better than sacrifice,
And to heed than the fat of rams.
[23] For rebellion *is as* the sin of witchcraft,
And stubbornness *is as* iniquity and idolatry.
Because you have rejected the word of the LORD,
He also has rejected you from *being* king."

Theresa Heflin

Letter Seventy-Eight

As you know, My love, from the story of Samuel and Saul, that it is My desire that you obey My every command — for it is better than any sacrifice. I demand total obedience. It is not a hard thing that I require. It is for your own good that you obey Me — for I Am God and I know all things. It is harmful to you to do anything that I do not want you to do. I want you to live in great peace and great joy — full of Victory and blessings. Obeying all My commands brings life to you and all your family for generations to come. Oh one that I love — you do obey Me — I am pleased with you — but you must never forget — never forget — obey everything I say. You will not understand many things at the time — but trust Me, precious one — trust Me completely — and obey — above all else — obey Me. I am taking good care of you. Remain in Me — sing for joy — for I give you many blessings. It is a time for joy, My love, for I am saying yes to everything you desire — for your heart is pure before Me and you seek My perfect will. I rejoice over you with much gladness! I love you, mighty warrior — oh My mighty warrior — I love you so.

Seventy-Nine

1 JOHN 3 NKJV

[14]We know that we have passed from death to life, because we love the brethren. He who does not love *his* brother abides in death. [15]Whoever hates his brother is a murderer, and you know that no murderer has eternal life abiding in him.

[16]By this we know love, because He laid down His life for us. And we also ought to lay down *our* lives for the brethren. [17]But whoever has this world's goods, and sees his brother in need, and shuts up his heart from him, how does the love of God abide in him?

[18]My little children, let us not love in word or in tongue, but in deed and in truth.

Theresa Heflin

Letter Seventy-Nine

Mighty warrior of Mine who represents Me – you must remain in Me – at all times – remain in Me. For what I require of you – you cannot do – it is impossible for you. My requirements are for you to love Me with all your heart, soul, mind, body, and strength. Then you must love your neighbor as yourself. Precious one, you cannot love another unless you are walking in the fullness of Me – for I Am Love – only My love can love the unlovable. It is My command to you that you love My people into My Kingdom. There is power in My love, mighty warrior. You can trust My love – for it is My love that will sustain you. So you must remain in Me – seek Me – cry out for wisdom and insight – for as you cry out – I will run to you! I will fill you with all of My love. I will give you a drink from My deep wells of water – My life flowing waters – filled with blessings of great peace and wonderful joy – oh the wonderful joy that I give you as you love more and more. Come, My love – let Me fill you with the fullness of My love so that you can love one another.

Eighty

MATTHEW 5 NKJV

³ "Blessed *are* the poor in spirit,
For theirs is the kingdom of heaven.
⁴ Blessed *are* those who mourn,
For they shall be comforted.
⁵ Blessed *are* the meek,
For they shall inherit the earth.
⁶ Blessed *are* those who hunger and thirst for righteousness,
For they shall be filled.
⁷ Blessed *are* the merciful,
For they shall obtain mercy.
⁸ Blessed *are* the pure in heart,
For they shall see God.
⁹ Blessed *are* the peacemakers,
For they shall be called sons of God.
¹⁰ Blessed *are* those who are persecuted for righteousness' sake,
For theirs is the kingdom of heaven.
¹¹"Blessed are you when they revile and persecute you, and say all kinds of evil against you falsely for My sake. ¹²Rejoice and be exceedingly glad, for great *is* your reward in heaven, for so they persecuted the prophets who were before you.

Letter Eighty

The heart that is pure – the heart that is open – the heart that is exposed to Me for cleansing is the pure in heart. Oh mighty warrior, as you come to Me – open – completely open – I reveal Myself to you – I personally reveal Myself to you – all of My love – all of My Glory – I will show you, My love. Continue to seek Me – continue to cry out for more – continue to ask Me to search you. I search you, My love – I cleanse you – I purify you – you have a pure heart before Me because I have given you My Son – My Beloved Son – My Son shed His blood for you so you could come to Me. Never doubt My love for you – never doubt My power – I give you My power through My love. I Am Love – I want you to have the power in My love. Remember – you must always forgive – pray for those who hurt you – for those who hurt you are hurting, My love. They need Me – they need you to pray for them. Pray for My people – My precious people – you will find healing – you will draw closer to Me as you pray one for another. Oh pray, My love – pray – for I am listening – I am listening – and I say yes to you!

Eighty-One

MATTHEW 18 NKJV

[21]Then Peter came to Him and said, "Lord, how often shall my brother sin against me, and I forgive him? Up to seven times?"

[22]Jesus said to him, "I do not say to you, up to seven times, but up to seventy times seven. [23]Therefore the kingdom of heaven is like a certain king who wanted to settle accounts with his servants. [24]And when he had begun to settle accounts, one was brought to him who owed him ten thousand talents. [25]But as he was not able to pay, his master commanded that he be sold, with his wife and children and all that he had, and that payment be made. [26]The servant therefore fell down before him, saying, 'Master, have patience with me, and I will pay you all.' [27]Then the master of that servant was moved with compassion, released him, and forgave him the debt.

[28]"But that servant went out and found one of his fellow servants who owed him a hundred denarii; and he laid hands on him and took *him* by the throat, saying, 'Pay me what you owe!' [29]So his fellow servant fell down at his feet and begged him, saying, 'Have patience with me, and I will pay you all.' [30]And he would not, but went and threw him into prison till he should pay the debt… [32]Then his master, after he had called him, said to him, 'You wicked servant! I forgave you all that debt because you begged me. [33]Should you not also have had compassion on your fellow servant, just as I had pity on you?' [34]And his master was angry, and delivered him to the torturers until he should pay all that was due to him.

[35]"So My heavenly Father also will do to you if each of you, from his heart, does not forgive his brother his trespasses."

Theresa Heflin

Letter Eighty-One

Oh mighty warrior, let Me tell you why you must forgive — you must forgive everyone that hurts you. To forgive one another is what I require. To walk in My full love is to forgive one another. One who loves Me so — do you want to walk in My fullness? Do you want My great peace? Do you really want to please Me? Then forgive from your heart, My love. Do you think that I do not know your heart? Cry out to Me — I will give you love one for another as you pray for them. This is good for you, My love. This will keep you from bitterness. Bitterness destroys the soul from My joy, My laughter, My love and My great peace. You must guard your heart, My love — for the evil one is looking for every opportunity to take away your peace — your great peace that only I can give. Let My tender, loving mercies flow from you. Let My kind forgiveness flow from you. Let My tender sweetness be revealed through you — at all times — under every circumstance — for you represent Me. Represent Me well! I have chosen you because I trust you. Love My people — My precious people — one that I adore.

Eighty-Two

1 JOHN 4 NKJV

[7]Beloved, let us love one another, for love is of God; and everyone who loves is born of God and knows God. [8]He who does not love does not know God, for God is love. [9]In this the love of God was manifested toward us, that God has sent His only begotten Son into the world, that we might live through Him. [10]In this is love, not that we loved God, but that He loved us and sent His Son *to be* the propitiation for our sins. [11]Beloved, if God so loved us, we also ought to love one another.

Theresa Heflin

Letter Eighty-Two

Oh mighty warrior, you refresh Me with your praises. Oh how I love to make you smile! My Spirit delights in you, mighty one that I have chosen. I love you so. Do you know? I Am God – Almighty God – I Am Your Creator – I breathed My love into you – oh I breathed deeply into you, one that represents Me. I live in you – I shine in you – I am pleased with you, My precious treasure – My heart beats one with you. I am pouring My blessings into you. I Am Love, mighty warrior – I Am Pure Perfect Love. I give you all of My love to serve My people – My precious people – they need Me, mighty warrior – they need Me – I send you to them, My love – I send you – I trust you, precious one – I trust you with them. Do you know that I am in love with you, My priceless treasure? Do you know how much I love you? I love you more than all that is – I love you more than all you can see or know – I love you – I love you – more than heaven and earth! I give you the fullness of Me! Go – love My people – let My love shine in you. Give them all of Me – for I give you all of Me – My blessed one.

Eighty-Three

EPHESIANS 4 NKJV

[25]Therefore, putting away lying, *"Let each one of you speak truth with his neighbor,"* for we are members of one another. [26]*"Be angry, and do not sin"*: do not let the sun go down on your wrath, [27]nor give place to the devil. [28]Let him who stole steal no longer, but rather let him labor, working with *his* hands what is good, that he may have something to give him who has need. [29]Let no corrupt word proceed out of your mouth, but what is good for necessary edification, that it may impart grace to the hearers. [30]And do not grieve the Holy Spirit of God, by whom you were sealed for the day of redemption. [31]Let all bitterness, wrath, anger, clamor, and evil speaking be put away from you, with all malice. [32]And be kind to one another, tenderhearted, forgiving one another, even as God in Christ forgave you.

Theresa Heflin

Letter Eighty-Three

Blessed are you, one who loves the unlovable. Blessed are you who hate the evil that abounds but loves My people. My people are bound in the darkness of evil, My love. You must pray for them for I love them so. Do not be discouraged in being kind to the unkind. They need Me, precious one – they need Me. Remain in Me – remain in My love – the power in My love heals – renews – refreshes and brings much joy and great peace. Oh one that loves Me so, I have placed you in the midst of the evil for a time. Show My love, tender heart – remain true to My commands – for I am with you. I give you the fullness of Me – and I Am God – I Am Your God who loves you so – and I Am Love. Trust Me, righteous one – My love breaks strongholds. I make a way when there seems to be no way. Praise Me – worship Me – keep your eyes on only Me – on heavenly things – and watch Me pave the way for you. Mighty warrior – never forget – you must never forget – I Am the Truth the Light and the Way. Lean on Me – only Me – love Me – love only Me – for I love you so and I take good care of you.

Eighty-Four

Matthew 9 NKJV

[35]Then Jesus went about all the cities and villages, teaching in their synagogues, preaching the gospel of the kingdom, and healing every sickness and every disease among the people. [36]But when He saw the multitudes, He was moved with compassion for them, because they were weary and scattered, like sheep having no shepherd. [37]Then He said to His disciples, "The harvest truly *is* plentiful, but the laborers *are* few. [38]Therefore pray the Lord of the harvest to send out laborers into His harvest."

John 4 NKJV

[35]Do you not say, 'There are still four months and *then* comes the harvest'? Behold, I say to you, lift up your eyes and look at the fields, for they are already white for harvest! [36]And he who reaps receives wages, and gathers fruit for eternal life, that both he who sows and he who reaps may rejoice together. [37]For in this the saying is true: 'One sows and another reaps.' [38]I sent you to reap that for which you have not labored; others have labored, and you have entered into their labors."

Theresa Heflin

Letter Eighty-Four

Mighty warrior, one that I love – oh one that I have chosen – now is the time, My love – now is the time. The season is here – it is harvest time, My love. Come – I bring you into My fields – come walk with Me – come talk with Me – come let Me shine in you – let the world see My Glory! Oh Mighty One – I have chosen you to represent Me. I created your heart – oh I created your heart – I love the heart I created in you. I created you to love Me. Oh how I love to hear you praise Me – oh how I love your worship to Me. You are My delight – all of heaven rejoices when you sing to Me. Oh how I love you, My mighty warrior – My creation – My bride – My separate holy one. I bless you, My love. Oh how I bless you! My smile is upon you in everything you do. I guide you – I lead you – I control you – I give you your desire for more of Me – for I love giving you more of Me. I Am Love – I Am Your love – I give you My love – love My people – My precious people. I am coming soon – oh I am coming soon to take you home with Me, My bride – come – rejoice with Me – blessed one – rejoice!

Eighty-Five

JOHN 17 NKJV

[13]But now I come to You, and these things I speak in the world, that they may have My joy fulfilled in themselves. [14]I have given them Your word; and the world has hated them because they are not of the world, just as I am not of the world. [15]I do not pray that You should take them out of the world, but that You should keep them from the evil one. [16]They are not of the world, just as I am not of the world. [17]Sanctify them by Your truth. Your word is truth. [18]As You sent Me into the world, I also have sent them into the world. [19]And for their sakes I sanctify Myself, that they also may be sanctified by the truth.

Theresa Heflin

Letter Eighty-Five

My precious one, I am loving you today. Today will be full of the overflow of Me. I give to you power – power in My love – My love – GOD – Almighty God's power. You will feel My abundance – you will enjoy much love from Me today. It will humble you beyond words – and I will smile on you even more. Oh mighty one that I have chosen to love Me – I love you so – experience Me – Almighty God – come – receive all of Me, My love – I give you all of Me. You do not belong to this earth – you belong only to Me. Keep your eyes on only Me – only My love – only My joy – only My sorrow – only My pain – only My deep peace – as you live in the fullness of Me. I strengthen you, My love – I will give you the strength to walk in the fullness of Me. I Am Your God Who Prepares You – I Am Your God Who Teaches You – I Am Your God Who Equips You for your service to Me. Remain in your total trust of Me – rely on only Me at all times in every instance about every thing – for I Am God – Almighty God – Creator of all that is and was and is to be and I am in control of you – oh precious one – I am in love with you – watch Me delight in you – My precious shining star!

Eighty-Six

PSALM 45 NKJV

[10] Listen, O daughter,
Consider and incline your ear;
Forget your own people also, and your father's house;
[11] So the King will greatly desire your beauty;
Because He *is* your Lord, worship Him.
[12] And the daughter of Tyre *will come* with a gift;
The rich among the people will seek your favor.

[13] The royal daughter *is* all glorious within *the palace;*
Her clothing *is* woven with gold.
[14] She shall be brought to the King in robes of many colors;
The virgins, her companions who follow her, shall be brought to You.
[15] With gladness and rejoicing they shall be brought;
They shall enter the King's palace.

Theresa Heflin

Letter Eighty-Six

I see your hunger for more of Me, mighty warrior. Oh I see you – I hear you – I will give you My words of love, for you love Me so. I created you to love Me so – oh how I love you – My creation – My beautiful one. I rejoice over you – I sing with you – I am delighting in you – oh how it delights Me to give you gifts – I give you joy – much joy – oh laugh with Me – dance with Me – sing to Me – for I Am Your God who is in love with you. Do you know why I whisper to you, My love? Do you know why I come in quietness – the still small voice – the voice of the quiet flowing of the rivers – it is Me, My love – it is Me – I come in the stillness, I whisper My love to you – you hear My whispers because you are close to My heart. You are close, My love – come closer – the closer you come – the more you will hear Me – for I love to whisper My love to you. Come, My love – let Me whisper how much I love you – I adore you – I am smiling on you. Oh one that I love – feel Me – feel My smile in you. Oh precious one – I am with you in every thing you do – for I enjoy you so! You please Me, mighty warrior – oh how you please Me!

Eighty-Seven

JOHN 15 NKJV

[11]"These things I have spoken to you, that My joy may remain in you, and *that* your joy may be full. [12]This is My commandment, that you love one another as I have loved you. [13]Greater love has no one than this, than to lay down one's life for his friends. [14]You are My friends if you do whatever I command you. [15]No longer do I call you servants, for a servant does not know what his master is doing; but I have called you friends, for all things that I heard from My Father I have made known to you. [16]You did not choose Me, but I chose you and appointed you that you should go and bear fruit, and *that* your fruit should remain, that whatever you ask the Father in My name He may give you. [17]These things I command you, that you love one another.

Theresa Heflin

Letter Eighty-Seven

Mighty warrior, I have placed a hedge of protection around you. The evil one cannot harm you. I have spoken! You will go in My power, you will go in all of My love, and you will go in the name of My Son — My beloved Son — who paid the price for you. I bless you, mighty warrior; I equip you, My chosen one in whom I love. The world cannot have you — you are Mine — only Mine — I will not share you — I will not! Remain in the fullness of Me — remain in My love — oh how I love to love you — oh how I enjoy our alone times — oh how I delight you. I love you, My creation, My precious priceless treasure. You must love one another through My love. It is the only way to walk in My fullness. Oh walk in the fullness of Me, My love — for it is better for you. Praise Me — adore Me — worship Me — love Me with all your heart, mind, body, soul, and strength — forgive one another — love one another — pray for one another — pray for those who persecute you. Come close — come to Me — pray to Me — I Am Your King who hears you. I Am Your King who answers you! I Am Your King — Your King — I say yes to you — because I want to — and I Am God — Almighty God — I can do whatever I choose!

Eighty-Eight

2 PETER 3

[1]Beloved, I now write to you this second epistle (in *both of* which I stir up your pure minds by way of reminder), [2]that you may be mindful of the words which were spoken before by the holy prophets, and of the commandment of us, the apostles of the Lord and Savior, [3]knowing this first: that scoffers will come in the last days, walking according to their own lusts, [4]and saying, "Where is the promise of His coming?

[8]But, beloved, do not forget this one thing, that with the Lord one day *is* as a thousand years, and a thousand years as one day. [9]The Lord is not slack concerning *His* promise, as some count slackness, but is longsuffering toward us, not willing that any should perish but that all should come to repentance.

Theresa Heflin

Letter Eighty-Eight

Precious one that I love, you have entered into My secret place. You are one with Me. You will weep with Me — you will feel My sorrow. I will love you deeply in My sorrow for My people — for My people keep rejecting Me, My love. So many think it is all a game — so many are playing in the midst of My time of judgment. I separate you from the world, My love. I choose you to pray for My people — My precious people. Pray for them! Cry out for them — for they are blind and do not see. Ask Me to open their eyes, precious one — ask Me to reveal Myself to them. Trust Me, mighty warrior — oh trust only Me, precious one. Only I — Almighty God — choose My people — you must pray for them. This is My command to you. Pray for My lost people — love them into My Kingdom! Do not be weary of doing good deeds! I Am Almighty God — Creator of all that is — all things are under My control — My eternal control! Mighty warrior, never forget — I love you so — I love to hear you pray for My precious people — I bless you, My love — I bless your family, My love — for I Am Your God who loves you so.

Eighty-Nine

1 CORINTHIANS 12 NKJV

[7]But the manifestation of the Spirit is given to each one for the profit *of all:* [8]for to one is given the word of wisdom through the Spirit, to another the word of knowledge through the same Spirit, [9]to another faith by the same Spirit, to another gifts of healings by the same Spirit, [10]to another the working of miracles, to another prophecy, to another discerning of spirits, to another *different* kinds of tongues, to another the interpretation of tongues. [11]But one and the same Spirit works all these things, distributing to each one individually as He wills.

Theresa Heflin

Letter Eighty-Nine

Mighty, mighty warrior, I strengthen you in My love today. Come – walk in My love today. Praise Me, precious one – for I am here to love you abundantly today – you are My precious, holy treasure. Oh how you please Me, My love! I shower you with blessings – I bring you gifts – oh – I have gifts, My precious one – I have gifts lovingly chosen just for you. You are My precious chosen one! Come into Me and let Me give you My gifts. I long to give them to you – oh how I long to give you more of Me! You have only just begun to see Me, My beautiful one. I am here to bless you – I bless you – I bless everything you touch – I bless all that you love – you are Mine – and I Am God – I give you the desires of your heart! Oh praise Me, precious one – for I Am Your God who says yes to you! You are in Me and I am in you – all of heaven rejoices with Me over you – oh if you only knew how much you are loved! Through My Precious Son – you are My precious one too! I give you all you need – I give you all you want! Remain in Me – love Me – love Me only – oh – love only Me, My love and watch and see what I can do! I will change the world for you! It is My world and I can do whatever I choose for you, My love – I say yes! Rejoice! Come – rejoice and praise Me!

Ninety

1 SAMUEL 18 NKJV

¹Now when he had finished speaking to Saul, the soul of Jonathan was knit to the soul of David, and Jonathan loved him as his own soul. ²Saul took him that day, and would not let him go home to his father's house anymore. ³Then Jonathan and David made a covenant, because he loved him as his own soul. ⁴And Jonathan took off the robe that *was* on him and gave it to David, with his armor, even to his sword and his bow and his belt.

HEBREWS 11 NKJV

⁵By faith Enoch was taken away so that he did not see death, *"and was not found, because God had taken him"*; for before he was taken he had this testimony, that he pleased God. ⁶But without faith *it is* impossible to please *Him,* for he who comes to God must believe that He is, and *that* He is a rewarder of those who diligently seek Him.

Theresa Heflin

Letter Ninety

Mighty warrior, I bring to you My chosen ones to encourage you along the path that I have prepared just for you. For I remember, My love, that you are but dust. I strengthen your mortal body in the fullness of My Holy Spirit. I give you a variety of My gems – My precious gems – on their own paths that I have prepared for them. I let you meet along the way for refreshment from the battles. Oh Mighty warrior – I do not leave you alone – I know your needs before you even ask. I prepare tables before you to dine and drink of My goodness. Oh precious, priceless love of Mine, I take good care of you. You must trust only Me – rejoice in Me – praise My Name – I am with you – I hear you – I do not take My eyes off of you. I am deeply in love with you. I created you to love Me – I created you to praise Me – I created you to worship Me. You must not worry – you must not fret – for I am among you – working all things for good for you. When you truly understand Me, you will rejoice in all things – for I do what is best for you. You are priceless to Me – I delight in you – oh how I love to bless you. I am pleased with you, My love.

Ninety-One

COLOSSIANS 3 NKJV

[12]Therefore, as *the* elect of God, holy and beloved, put on tender mercies, kindness, humility, meekness, longsuffering; [13]bearing with one another, and forgiving one another, if anyone has a complaint against another; even as Christ forgave you, so you also *must do.* [14]But above all these things put on love, which is the bond of perfection. [15]And let the peace of God rule in your hearts, to which also you were called in one body; and be thankful. [16]Let the word of Christ dwell in you richly in all wisdom, teaching and admonishing one another in psalms and hymns and spiritual songs, singing with grace in your hearts to the Lord. [17]And *whatever* you do in word or deed, *do* all in the name of the Lord Jesus, giving thanks to God the Father through Him.

Theresa Heflin

Letter Ninety-One

It is because of you, mighty warrior, one that I love, that I do not regret My creation! Oh how you please Me so! Remain in My fullness, mighty one in whom I have chosen – remain in Me – for I strengthen you to love Me more. Pour My wonderful love into My people, precious one – oh My precious people. You are chosen to represent Me – you are chosen to love them – oh how I love to watch you love them! All of heaven rejoices over you – I sing over you – I rejoice over you! Oh how I love you so! Keep your eyes on only Me – keep your thoughts on only Me – for I tell you new things – I tell you My plan – I reveal Myself to you! You are My dear friend in whom I trust. I trust you with My love, mighty warrior. Did you know I trust you with My love? Do you know how beautiful you are to Me, My lovely one? You are My beautiful creation! I laugh with you and I cry with you – just as you laugh and cry with My precious children I have given to you. You are very precious to Me – you are very dear to Me. Never forget, My love, I am here – come to Me – I will give you rest. Drop all your cares on Me! I answer you – now – come – rejoice – for I love you – and I Am God – Almighty God – and I Am Good!

Ninety-Two

DANIEL 9 NKJV

²⁰Now while I *was* speaking, praying, and confessing my sin and the sin of my people Israel, and presenting my supplication before the LORD my God for the holy mountain of my God, ²¹yes, while I *was* speaking in prayer, the man Gabriel, whom I had seen in the vision at the beginning, being caused to fly swiftly, reached me about the time of the evening offering. ²²And he informed *me,* and talked with me, and said, "O Daniel, I have now come forth to give you skill to understand. ²³At the beginning of your supplications the command went out, and I have come to tell *you,* for you *are* greatly beloved; therefore consider the matter, and understand the vision:

DANIEL 9 NLT

"Daniel, I have come here to give you insight and understanding. ²³The moment you began praying, a command was given. And now I am here to tell you what it was, for you are very precious to God. Listen carefully so that you can understand the meaning of your vision.

Theresa Heflin

Letter Ninety-Two

Oh mighty warrior, you are rare – you are My prized possession. Oh how you please Me, My love. Do you know who I am? Do you really know? I Am the Ancient of Days – I Am GOD – the One and Only Creator of heaven and earth and all that is within! Because of My great love for you, My beautiful creation – My rare gem of all gems – I gave you My Beloved Son – My Only Son – who willingly, with much love – suffered for you. Now – because of Him – you may spend eternity with Me! Oh beautiful one – do you know how much I love you? I have given you My Holy Spirit! My Holy Spirit hovered over the waters from the beginning, precious one. He carries with Him all of My power – all of My comfort – all of My goodness – He prays for you, My righteous one – My holy one – He cares for you – He is with you always – taking good care of you! Oh precious one – made in My image – I give you everything – I have given you all of Me – give to My people – My precious people – oh one that I love – love one another in the fullness of Me – and watch and see what I can do!

Ninety-Three

1 PETER 5 NKJV

[6]Therefore humble yourselves under the mighty hand of God, that He may exalt you in due time, [7]casting all your care upon Him, for He cares for you.

[8]Be sober, be vigilant; because your adversary the devil walks about like a roaring lion, seeking whom he may devour. [9]Resist him, steadfast in the faith, knowing that the same sufferings are experienced by your brotherhood in the world. [10]But may the God of all grace, who called us to His eternal glory by Christ Jesus, after you have suffered a while, perfect, establish, strengthen, and settle *you*. [11]To Him *be* the glory and the dominion forever and ever. Amen.

Theresa Heflin

Letter Ninety-Three

I enjoy living in you, My precious one. I am refreshed by your love for Me. I am so pleased with you, My beautiful creation. You hunger for more of Me — I give you your hunger and thirst. Oh mighty warrior, hunger for more of Me! I am here to answer you! Oh how it pleases Me to draw you into Me. You cannot survive without Me! Draw deep from My well — drink deeply of My love — for I fill you to overflowing! Remain in My love — oh remain deeply in My love — for you must love one another. As the evil escalates, My love — I pour Myself stronger into you. I will sustain you with My love. There is power in My love. There is Victory in My love! Never forget — never forget — I love you — love Me with your every thought — I desire all of you. Remain in My love — for that is where you please Me. Oh please Me, My beautiful one — for I Am Your God who loves you so. Be kind to one another — pray for one another — do not let the evil one take away the joy I give you. Remain in the fullness of My love — I Am Your King who protects you.

Ninety-Four

COLOSSIANS 2 NKJV

²that their hearts may be encouraged, being knit together in love, and *attaining* to all riches of the full assurance of understanding, to the knowledge of the mystery of God, both of the Father and of Christ, ³in whom are hidden all the treasures of wisdom and knowledge.

COLOSSIANS 2 NLT

Then God made you alive with Christ, for he forgave all our sins. ¹⁴He canceled the record of the charges against us and took it away by nailing it to the cross. ¹⁵In this way, he disarmed the spiritual rulers and authorities. He shamed them publicly by his victory over them on the cross.

Theresa Heflin

Letter Ninety-Four

Oh mighty warrior, don't you know – I live in you. You do as I say – you go where I lead – you trust Me – you hear Me – you know My voice – My creation, My beautiful one. Never forget – I live in you. I Am Almighty God. In the fullness of Me – My Holy Spirit dwells in you. I give you all My power through My love, mighty warrior. All of what you are – all of what I give you is through the power of My love. My love does not harm you, precious one. My love is pure – My love is patient – My love endures – My love is kind – My love pours through you – you must give My love to My people – My precious people. They live in darkness, holy one – they live in bondage – oh weep with Me – for their souls are lost. Love them, My love – for I give you all of Me to go forth and love them. Evil pervades them and has them bound by forces that My love can break. Pray for them – love them – bring them into My Kingdom – for I am coming soon, My love. Worship Me – praise Me – thank Me continuously – for I Am Your King who has saved you and pulled you out of the darkness. All praise and honor and Glory to My Name – for I Am Your God who is in love with you.

Ninety-Five

2 CORINTHIANS 9 NKJV

[6]But this *I say:* He who sows sparingly will also reap sparingly, and he who sows bountifully will also reap bountifully. [7]*So let* each one *give* as he purposes in his heart, not grudgingly or of necessity; for God loves a cheerful giver. [8]And God *is* able to make all grace abound toward you, that you, always having all sufficiency in all *things,* may have an abundance for every good work.
[10]Now may He who supplies seed to the sower, and bread for food, supply and multiply the seed you have *sown* and increase the fruits of your righteousness, [11]while *you are* enriched in everything for all liberality, which causes thanksgiving through us to God.

Theresa Heflin

Letter Ninety-Five

Rejoice in Me, mighty warrior – for I have given you the gift of giving! Your cup will always overflow in the giving, My precious one. I give you those to love in the giving. Righteous one – you are giving to Me when you meet the needs of the poor – the starving ones. Precious one – you are serving Me when I send you the elderly who cannot care for themselves anymore. I bless you, My love – bless My precious people. You are loving Me and pleasing Me when you care for My children – oh My precious children! Care for them greatly – for they are closest to My heart! Oh mighty warrior – remain in My love – I will teach you – I will show you – I will bless you. I trust you, My love – I will show you the work of My plans for you. Oh mighty warrior – you will love the plans I have for you! I smile upon you – I bring laughter to you – I fill you with great joy! I bless all your children! I bless all your grandchildren! I have given you many children and many grandchildren, My love – and I bless them! You are the reason I sing!

Ninety-Six

ISAIAH 58 NKJV

¹⁰ *If* you extend your soul to the hungry
And satisfy the afflicted soul,
Then your light shall dawn in the darkness,
And your darkness shall *be* as the noonday.
¹¹ The LORD will guide you continually,
And satisfy your soul in drought,
And strengthen your bones;
You shall be like a watered garden,
And like a spring of water, whose waters do not fail.

Theresa Heflin

Letter Ninety-Six

I have entrusted My people into your care, mighty warrior. You are the one I have chosen. I live in you, precious one. I guide you into My truth. I Am Love and I give My love to you and make you holy. You represent Me in your love one for another. Serve My people, precious one. It is My plan — it is by My design that you help one another. Only then, My love, will you remain free from the clutches of the evil one. It is only through My love, one that I trust, that you can live in My great peace and joy. I give you rivers of great peace and joy when you remain in My love. The power is in My love — your strength is in My joy. Rest in the peace I give you. You represent Me, mighty warrior. I am pleased with you — I am pleased with your service to Me. But, you must never forget — never forget, My love — you cannot live without Me — all that you are — all that you have — I have given to you to serve Me. I want you to worship Me — I want you to praise Me — I want more of your time to spend alone with Me. I want all of you, My love — for I have given you all of Me.

Ninety-Seven

ACTS 26 NKJV

[15]So I said, 'Who are You, Lord?' And He said, 'I am Jesus, whom you are persecuting. [16]But rise and stand on your feet; for I have appeared to you for this purpose, to make you a minister and a witness both of the things which you have seen and of the things which I will yet reveal to you. [17]I will deliver you from the *Jewish* people, as well as *from* the Gentiles, to whom I now send you, [18]to open their eyes, *in order* to turn *them* from darkness to light, and *from* the power of Satan to God, that they may receive forgiveness of sins and an inheritance among those who are sanctified by faith in Me.'

Theresa Heflin

Letter Ninety-Seven

Do not be discouraged, precious one that I love. I hear your every thought — I hear you with much tenderness and you have My full attention at all times. I know every breath you take — I have given to you those that you love. It is My desire that you love them. It is My desire that you pray for them. It is My desire that you seek My perfect will for their lives. Continue bringing them to Me, My love — for it is My urging in your soul for them. They are very precious to Me, mighty warrior. I have great plans for them. Continue to love them — continue to bring them before Me — continue in your service to Me, precious one. You please Me when you love My people. I answer you, My love — I answer you with great pleasure! You are My special one that I have chosen. It is My Spirit in you, My love that draws them to Me. You must remain in the fullness of Me. Remain deep in My love — cry out for wisdom and insight — cry out for more of Me! Let Me reveal the fullness of Me to you. Let Me show you how much I love you! I love you so, come — let Me love you more!

Ninety-Eight

ACTS 13 NKJV

[1]Now in the church that was at Antioch there were certain prophets and teachers: Barnabas, Simeon who was called Niger, Lucius of Cyrene, Manaen who had been brought up with Herod the tetrarch, and Saul. [2]As they ministered to the Lord and fasted, the Holy Spirit said, "Now separate to Me Barnabas and Saul for the work to which I have called them." [3]Then, having fasted and prayed, and laid hands on them, they sent *them* away.

ISAIAH 65 NKJV

[18] But be glad and rejoice forever in what I create;
For behold, I create Jerusalem *as* a rejoicing,
  And her people a joy.
[19] I will rejoice in Jerusalem,
  And joy in My people;

Letter Ninety-Eight

Mighty warrior, oh My mighty warrior — I love the way you trust Me — oh I love your heart! You are in perfect harmony with Me, My love. We are one — blessed one. You know My voice, righteous, holy one — obey Me always. There is much joy and great peace in you because you rely on Me — you depend on Me — you trust Me in all things — oh precious one — that is what pleases Me. I am so pleased with you, My mighty warrior. Oh how I love you so! Continue in your love for Me, one who trusts Me so. Remain in My love — continually seek Me — for I have more for you, My love. Oh, I have so much more for you. Shine for Me, My love. Reveal My love to them, My precious treasure. Let them see My peace, My great peace. Let them see My joy! You are Mine — you are completely Mine! Everything you say — everything you do — everywhere you go — is for Me — to Me — about Me — serving Me — that is My perfect will! You represent Me — you love Me with your thoughts — you are Mine — I bless everything you do — I will keep you humble — I protect you from the evil one, My love. Go in the confidence of My love for you — for it is great, My love!

Ninety-Nine

ISAIAH 40 NKJV

²⁸ Have you not known?
Have you not heard?
The everlasting God, the LORD,
The Creator of the ends of the earth,
Neither faints nor is weary.
His understanding is unsearchable.
²⁹ He gives power to the weak,
And to *those who have* no might He increases strength.
³⁰ Even the youths shall faint and be weary,
And the young men shall utterly fall,
³¹ But those who wait on the LORD
Shall renew *their* strength;
They shall mount up with wings like eagles,
They shall run and not be weary,
They shall walk and not faint.

Theresa Heflin

Letter Ninety-Nine

Mighty warrior, encourage each other along your path. I have designed it – it is My plan – that you help each other along the way. When you see one of Mine discouraged and facing a suffering, help them, My love. Pray one for another – share the encouragement of the Good News – remind them that I have won and the Victory is Mine! If they need supplies – furnish their supplies – support each other in all ways for all seasons. I give to you – give to them – I bless you – bless them – for that is what pleases Me. I give you special gifts – special talents – share them – all work together in My body – then the Good News is spread throughout My world! Love My people as I have loved you. Work diligently for the time is short! Remain in My love so that you will bear much fruit – for that is My desire – you please Me when you bear much fruit. Oh precious one, you cannot do this without Me. Seek Me – cry out for more of Me – I will come – I will show you – I will teach you – for I Am Your God who loves you so.

One Hundred

PSALM 36 NKJV

[7] How precious *is* Your loving kindness, O God!
Therefore the children of men put their trust under the shadow of Your wings.
[8] They are abundantly satisfied with the fullness of Your house,
And You give them drink from the river of Your pleasures.
[9] For with You *is* the fountain of life;
In Your light we see light.

[10] Oh, continue Your loving kindness to those who know You,
And Your righteousness to the upright in heart.

Theresa Heflin

Letter One Hundred

Oh tender heart that loves Me so – I adore you – I smile on you, My love – oh how I love to hear you worship Me. I love the sound of My Name on your lips – I love you, My beautiful creation – I love your tender heart. I am so pleased with you, My precious creation – I am so pleased with you. Rest in Me, My love – come deep into My secret place and let Me refresh you in My love. You are very precious to Me, My chosen one. I take good care of you. I hear your heart – I hear your whispers – I see your face – I feel your love – I feel your pain – I feel you, My love – we are one. Come – I am here to love you – I rejoice over you – I sing to you – I Am Your King who is in love with you! You are Mine – you belong to Me – adore Me – worship Me – thank Me – for I love to watch you – I love to hear you – I love your voice – I love your soul – I am so in love with you! I never get tired of you – never – oh come to Me – delight Me with all of you – smile for Me – sing to Me – whisper to Me – think of Me – love Me – love Me more – cry out for more of Me – I have so much more to give you, My love – come – receive of Me – let Me give you more!

Poem

I am your God, your Savior, and your King
I want you to live with Me through all eternity.
Come walk with Me – your Savior and your Guide
I am with you always – I never leave your side.
I paid the price for you as I hung on the tree
It was a cruel tree – the price I paid for thee.
Come walk with Me – your Savior and your Friend
for I am the only one that stays 'til the end.
You are the one I chose to adore
and love and cherish with gifts galore!
Come walk with Me – My precious priceless treasure
for it is you, My love, that gives Me much pleasure.
I hold you tight each morning and each night
and in-between with much delight.
Come walk with Me – My beautiful bride
I am your One and Only standing by your side.
I watch you constantly with My careful eye –
Just as I do My sparrows that fall from My sky.
Come fly with Me, My beautiful one
for I have given you My Beloved Son!

Theresa Heflin

Helpful Bible Verses

Situation	Bible Verse
Afraid	II Timothy 1:7 Hebrews 13:5-6
Angry	Ephesians 4:26-27 James 1:19-20
Anxious	Matthew 6:19-34 Philippians 4:6-7
Crisis	Matthew 6:23-34 Hebrews 4:16
Depressed	Romans 8:18,31-39 James 1:2-4
Discouraged	II Corinth 4:8-18 Philippians 4:4-7
Doubting	Matthew 21:21-22 Hebrews 4:1-3
Lonely	Hebrews 13:5-6 John 15:4-11
Peace	John 14:1, 25-27 Romans 5:1-5
Sick	James 5:13-16 1 Peter 2:24
Sorrowful	John 14 II Corinthians 1:3-4
Tempted	James 1:12-16 I Corinth 10:12-14 I Peter 5:6-9
Weary	Matthew 11:28-30 Galatians 6:9-10

About the Author

I gave my heart to Christ when I was nine years old in 1963. My dad was serving in Viet Nam at the time – giving me an early start in realizing the need to pray daily. I can remember praying every night for God to please let my dad live and come back home to us…and he did. My dad went on to be with our Lord in 1989.

I married and God gave me a beautiful daughter, Allison, who has brought me much joy as Stephen and "little Stephen" have entered my life. Later, I married again and God gave me a beautiful daughter, Missy, who has brought me much joy as Gene and "Parker and John" have entered my life.

My husband and I were part owners of a hospital in Waverly, TN prior to retiring. I remember feeling the need to spice up my life when I became forty. I was appeased when I received my pilot's license. However, my husband wouldn't fly with me because he said he didn't have a death wish. So, I sold my little Mooney and was satisfied that I had accomplished that feat. When I turned fifty, it didn't bother me at all.

After nearly twenty years of marriage, I am now a widow. During the death of my husband, Dick, my walk with God has grown into a deeper level of searching and devotion. During the last four years of searching for more, I have entered into a place within my heart that allows me to receive God's unfailing love. He created us to not only love Him, but to become more aware of our Creator's enormous love for us. These letters are given to me every morning after I have studied my Bible and have asked God to reveal Himself to me.

As I was walking in the park one day, I felt the sweet tender voice inside of me whisper, "Give my love letters to the world." These letters are for you, personally, the precious people, God's great creation. I believe with all my heart that God wants each of us to know Him intimately. Although these letters are personal to me, they will also be personal to you, for they are inspired by God.

Theresa Heflin

Comments

"Daily bible study for couples such as us is an important way to keep that sacred bond of marriage. *Love Letters* has given us the motivation and encouragement to make time each day to spend together and to study and appreciate the messages God intended for us. Thank you to Theresa for inspiring us to better our lives. She has truly been called upon in a special way to spread God's word."

Andy & Michelle Nichols

New Johnsonville, TN

"Everyone should and will be inspired as they read these letters. As I searched the scriptures and read the letters, no matter what I might have been facing for that day, God's Word was there for me to get a grip with His inspired Word. I draw closer to Him daily. Theresa, you are so inspiring, I love you, sis."

Jerry Lane

McEwen, TN

"The "Love Letters from God" will bless you immensely. Chose one, in any order, and you will be surprised how close to your heart the message will reach. This is the second collection of many to come. I can hardly wait for the next installment."

Ron Means
Trinity Assembly of God
Lawton, Oklahoma

Theresa Heflin